Victorian Christmas

Bobbie Kalman
Illustrations by Barbara Bedell

Crabtree Publishing Company

HISTORIC

COMMUNITIES

Created by Bobbie Kalman

For my dear friend Karen Vernal
May peace and love always be with you.

Editor-in-Chief
Bobbie Kalman

Research
April Fast
Hannelore Sotzek

Writing team
Bobbie Kalman
April Fast

Managing editor
Lynda Hale

Editors
Niki Walker
Greg Nickles
Petrina Gentile

Computer design
Lynda Hale

Separations and film
Dot 'n Line Image Inc.

Printer
Worzalla Publishing Company

Crabtree Publishing Company

350 Fifth Avenue
Suite 3308
New York
N.Y. 10118

360 York Road, RR 4
Niagara-on-the-Lake
Ontario, Canada
L0S 1J0

73 Lime Walk
Headington
Oxford OX3 7AD
United Kingdom

Cataloging in Publication Data
Kalman, Bobbie, 1947-
     Victorian Christmas
(Historic communities series)
Includes index.
ISBN 0-86505-430-4 (library bound) ISBN 0-86505-460-6 (pbk.)
This book examines Christmas traditions that began or were revived during the Victorian era, including Christmas trees and decorations, gift-giving, caroling, and other less well-known customs.

1. Christmas - United States - History - 19th century - Juvenile literature. I. Bedell, Barbara. II. Title. III. Series: Kalman, Bobbie, 1947-   . Historic communities. 1. Christmas - Canada - History - 19th century - Juvenile literature. I. Bedell, Barbara. II. Title. III. Series: Kalman, Bobbie, 1947-   . Historic communities.

GT4987.15.K3 1996   j394.2'663   LC 96-26735
                                                          CIP

Contents

Victorian Christmas

Christmas is a religious holiday honoring the birth of Jesus Christ, whom Christians believe to be the Son of God. In the early 1800s, people in North America celebrated Christmas by attending church and sharing a quiet meal with family and a few friends. Gift-giving was not a big part of Christmas celebrations. If a child received a present, it was a piece of fruit, a handmade toy, or an article of clothing.

The Victorian era

Christmas celebrations changed during the Victorian era. The Victorian era was the period of time between 1837 and 1901, when Queen Victoria ruled Britain. During this time in North America, factories began producing merchandise that made life easier, and people started earning more money. Christmas festivities grew as people had the time and money to celebrate, put up fancy decorations, and buy gifts for their loved ones.

A time for children

Until the early 1800s, parents believed that children would become spoiled if they received too much love and attention. Queen Victoria helped change these beliefs. She and her husband were very affectionate with their children, especially at Christmastime.

Newspapers and magazines showed pictures of the royal family celebrating Christmas with a decorated tree and gifts beneath it for the children. Children in North America were soon receiving gifts and extra attention from their parents.

During the Victorian era, Christmas became a special time for children. They looked forward to trimming the tree and receiving presents.

Queen Victoria's husband, Prince Albert, helped make the Christmas tree popular in Britain and North America. He brought the custom of decorating a Christmas tree from Germany, his homeland. In 1850, a picture of the royal family gathered around a candle-lit tree appeared in an American magazine. People were quick to imitate the royal family and, soon, Christmas trees were found in almost every home.

Decorating for Christmas

Victorian homes were beautifully decorated with bold wallpaper, lace curtains, richly colored drapes, layers of tablecloths, and ornately carved wooden furniture. At Christmastime, these houses looked even more wonderful!

People began decorating their homes weeks before Christmas Day. On the front porch, evergreen branches were tied to railings and draped above the doorway. A wreath made of pine boughs, pine cones, berries, and dried fruit was hung on the front door to welcome guests. The feeling of the outdoors was brought inside the home. Boughs of fir, spruce, and other evergreens were hung on walls and doors. Fireplace mantels, windows, and staircase railings were draped with garlands of holly, ivy, pine cones, and flowers.

The Advent wreath

The Advent wreath was placed on the dining-room table. It held four candles to mark the four weeks before Christmas. Each candle had its own meaning: faith, joy, love, and peace. One pink candle was lit on the first Sunday. Each Sunday after that, another pink candle was lit. The purple candle was lit on the last Sunday.

Decking the halls, walls, and windows

Every room in the house was decorated. Candles twinkled from the windows as if to light the way for the baby Jesus, who is also called the Christ Child. Christmas stockings hung from the fireplace mantel, awaiting treats and gifts. Even bedrooms were decked out for the holidays. Sprigs of greenery secured with bows were placed above the windows. Red ribbons were tied above pictures and, in some homes, Christmas dolls that looked like angels were placed in the windows and on the tree.

Nativity scenes

Nativity scenes were displayed in many Victorian homes. A Nativity scene is a group of small figurines set up to look like the stable in Bethlehem, where Jesus was born. Nativity scenes include a manger and figures of the Christ Child, his mother Mary, her husband Joseph, the Three Wise Men, and various farm animals.

The Christmas tree

The most important Christmas decoration in the house was the Christmas tree. It was set up on Christmas Eve and taken down on January 6th, the twelfth day of Christmas.

Legend has it that the first Christmas tree was decorated by Martin Luther in Germany. One Christmas Eve, Martin Luther went for a walk in the forest. Looking up, he noticed the stars twinkling around the snow-covered treetops, and the sight filled him with wonder. He brought a fir tree home to his family and placed on its branches candles that shone like stars.

The Victorian tree on page 9 is decorated with wonderful miniatures. With a friend, make a list of all the objects you see on the tree and then compare your lists. Who found the most decorations?

The perfect spot

Families searched for the perfect tree, cut it down, and placed it on a small table in the **parlor**. The parlor was the most richly decorated room in the house. It was a formal room used for family gatherings and entertaining guests. Everyone was sure to see the beautiful tree in this special room!

The early Victorian tree

The early Victorian Christmas trees were decorated with fruits, nuts, pine cones, and small homemade gifts. Tiny hand-stitched dolls and children's mittens added a personal touch, and treats such as small toys and sugar cookies delighted children. Hand-dipped candles shone from the branches, which were draped with strings of popcorn and berries. A star twinkled from the top of the tree to remind everyone of the Christmas star that led the Wise Men to Jesus.

Later Victorian trees

The later trees were much fancier than the earlier ones. Year after year, more elaborate decorations were added. The tree was showered with candles and miniatures of furniture, musical instruments, toys, fans, purses, and books. A Christmas doll or angel was also placed on the tree.

Christmas ornaments

By the late 1800s, many types of store-bought ornaments were hung on the Christmas tree. **Gewgaws** were small, inexpensive items that added color and sparkle. Gewgaws included candies wrapped in shiny paper, gold-painted nuts, and little birds made of colored paper or yarn. Candy canes and ribbon candy were also considered to be gewgaws.

Dresdens were ornaments that looked like metal but were actually made of cardboard. The cardboard was painted silver, gold, or copper. Some popular Dresdens were shaped like instruments, animals, and trains. Most of these ornaments were hung on the tree, but flat Dresdens were also pasted into scrapbooks.

German-made blown-glass balls, called kugels, were among the first Christmas ornaments to be sold in North American shops.

Sebnitz *ornaments were made of cotton batting covered with thin, crinkled wire and punched metal. They came in the shape of cradles, animals, boats, and carriages.*

Cornucopias *were shaped like cones and held candies, fruit, and nuts. Mesh bags also held small gifts and candies. Some were simple drawstring bags, but others were shaped like small stockings or Santas. The colors of the candies showed through the mesh.*

People collected colorful cardboard pictures of angels, children, and Santas. These decorations came to be known as "scraps" and were pasted into scrapbooks. Some scraps were cut out at the factory and sold as ready-made ornaments. Others were bought in sheets and made into ornaments at home.

German-made wax ornaments were popular and came in such forms as angels, children, animals, and fruit. They were decorated with cardboard, plaster, spun glass, cloth, and ribbon.

Père Nöel was the French Father Christmas.

The Russian settlers called St. Nicholas Koyla.

Swedish settlers pictured their Santa carrying a sheaf of wheat or barley.

Pelznickel was one name for the German Santa. He was also called Kriss Kringle by some German settlers.

The Dutch St. Nicholas, or Sinter Klaas, dressed in a bishop's robe and hat and rode a white horse.

Thomas Nast's drawing of Santa, shown left, looked like a combination of St. Nicholas and an elf, shown right. Instead of riding a horse or goat, this Santa Claus had a sleigh and eight reindeer.

So many Santas!

When settlers came to North America, they brought different ideas about Santa Claus with them. Many European children believed St. Nicholas brought them gifts. St. Nicholas was a fourteenth century bishop who gave gold to poor children. He was also known as Sinter Klaas, Pelznickel, Kriss Kringle, Père Nöel, and Father Christmas. St. Nicholas not only had different names, he also had various ways of dressing and traveling.

In 1823, Clement Moore helped create another look for St. Nick. He described Santa in his poem "A Visit From St. Nicholas," which is now called " 'Twas the Night Before Christmas." Working from Moore's description, an artist named Thomas Nast drew illustrations of a round-bellied, jolly St. Nicholas, who looked a lot like today's Santa Claus.

The British Father Christmas rode a goat.

13

Gifts for children

In the early 1800s, children received Christmas presents only from their parents. These Christmas gifts included handmade toys, hand-sewn clothes, and knitted socks, scarves, and mittens.

More stores, more gifts

During the Victorian era, gift-giving became an important part of Christmas celebrations. Stories were written about the virtues of giving presents, and newspapers ran articles on how to choose gifts. City stores began selling a wide variety of goods. Many parents had extra money to spend, so they began buying their children's Christmas gifts instead of making them.

On Christmas morning, children found presents piled on the parlor table and hung on the tree. The most common gifts included wind-up toys, board games, and dolls. Rocking horses, sleds, detailed dollhouses, and miniature zoos were also popular gifts.

A CHRISTMAS C

A Hearty Christmas Greeting!

Christmas cards

here were two main reasons why people did not send Christmas greetings in the early part of the nineteenth century: there were no Christmas cards for sale, and sending anything in the mail was like making a collect telephone call—the person who received the letter had to pay its postage. People did not want their friends to be obliged to pay for a Christmas greeting. When the post office started charging the sender instead of the receiver, people were less hesitant about mailing greeting cards to friends.

Fine-art cards

The first fine-art Christmas cards printed in North America were made by Louis Prang in the mid-1870s. Some of these cards had Christmas images, but many simply showed winter or country scenes. Pictures of children, angels, and birds were also popular. Before long, other printers produced beautiful cards as well. With millions of Christmas cards being printed each year, they became less expensive to buy, and more people began sending them.

The cards on these pages are samples of Louis Prang Christmas cards. In the late 1800s, his cards became so popular that almost five million were produced each year!

A time for parties, a time for love

he Christmas season was filled with good cheer. The weeks before Christmas were spent preparing and socializing. Small **socials**, or parties, brought together friends and neighbors to celebrate the season.

Home for the holidays

By the mid-1800s, improved roads and new railways made it easier for people to travel long distances. Family members living in different parts of the country were able to spend Christmas together, and these reunions made Christmastime even more special.

Visiting friends

During the Victorian era, **paying calls** was a popular custom. To pay a call meant to visit someone at their home. Calls were made year round, but it was especially important to visit friends at Christmastime. Bachelors called on unmarried women, and families went to the homes of friends and relatives.

Christmas parties

Over the Christmas season, wealthy families hosted lavish parties in ballrooms decorated with garlands, flowers, and candles. A band played festive music while guests, dressed in their fanciest clothing, danced the night away.

Christmas was considered a romantic time of year, and many weddings were held between Christmas and New Year's Day. Christmas week was the perfect time for weddings because homes were already decorated, and people had plenty of free time to enjoy these special events.

Christmas Eve

On Christmas Eve, households buzzed with excitement. The tree was set up and lovingly decorated. People often played charades, sang and danced to music played on the piano, or listened to someone read a Christmas tale. Children, wearing homemade costumes, performed Christmas plays that they had spent hours rehearsing.

Hay rides

In the country, many families went on hay rides. A wagon, piled high with bales of hay, drove slowly as its passengers sipped hot apple cider and sang Christmas carols. In the city, people rode through the streets and parks on sleighs or in carriages.

Scary stories

When night fell and the parlor fireplace dimmed, it was time to tell stories. Ghost stories were especially popular, and people took turns telling them. When a storyteller began reciting a tale, a bundle of sticks was thrown into the fire. The storyteller's tale had to last until the sticks stopped burning.

Evening church services

Many families attended nighttime church services such as Midnight Mass. The churches were decorated with evergreen boughs, and welcoming candles glowed in their windows. Church bells rang, and the streets buzzed with friendly chatter as neighbors and strangers gathered to celebrate the birth of Jesus Christ.

Bells rang out on Christmas Day

Christmas morning was alive with celebration and music, as the sound of church bells filled the air. Children awoke in the early light of dawn, anxious to empty their Christmas stockings. After breakfast, families dressed in their finest clothes and went to church.

When they came home from church, the children opened their "Christmas boxes," or gifts. Then, with much excitement, they presented their parents with small gifts or homemade Christmas cards called "Christmas pieces."

The groaning board

Christmas dinner was a huge meal that included many special dishes. The entire family sat at a table loaded with foods such as goose, turkey, ham, corn, yams, potatoes, stuffing, cranberry sauce, and gravy. Wines, cakes, and candies were also crammed onto the table. There was so much food that the table boards "groaned" under the weight of it all!

The plum pudding

The plum pudding was the highlight of the Christmas feast. It was a tasty dessert that was prepared five Sundays before Christmas, on **Stir-Up Sunday**. On this day, each family member took a turn stirring the pudding. People believed that if they made a wish while stirring the pudding, the wish would come true.

When the mixture was ready, it was put into a cloth bag and hung up until Christmas Day. Before being served, the pudding was boiled in water for four to five hours. Warm brandy was then poured over it and lit. The flaming treat, topped with a sprig of holly, was carried proudly to the table as the last dish of the day.

After-dinner celebrations

After the huge meal, people danced and played games. Later that night, decorated sleighs or carriages carried visitors from house to house. In northern regions, people went skating or found a snow-covered hill for tobogganing.

Parlor games

Favorite Christmas games included Blind Man's Buff, The Cobweb Game, and Bag and Stick. In the game of Bag and Stick, a paper bag filled with treats was hung from the ceiling. As shown in the picture, one person was blindfolded, turned around several times, and given a stick with which to hit the bag. If the first child could not break open the bag, another child was given a chance. When the bag was finally torn, the candies inside fell to the floor. Everyone scrambled to grab as many treats as they could!

Christmas traditions

During the Victorian era, people enjoyed many new Christmas activities that soon became traditions. They also revived customs that had not been practiced for hundreds of years.

Christmas stockings

The custom of hanging stockings on Christmas Eve became popular during the Victorian era. At first, most children simply hung an everyday sock by the fireplace. Some had special stockings that had been handmade just for them.

Christmas stockings became so popular that factories started producing them. Wealthier children found their stocking bulging with toys and candies. Most children, however, found theirs stuffed with fruit and nuts.

Pantomimes

Pantomimes were special plays for children. They were staged during the Christmas season, when students were on vacation. Most pantomimes were based on popular fairy tales. Children were dazzled by the stories, beautiful costumes, and lavish sets.

Christmas crackers

Christmas crackers were invented during the Victorian era. Crackers are rolled pieces of paper tied at each end, and when they are tugged apart by one or two people, there is a bang. This loud snapping noise is not the best part of the cracker, however. Inside are treats, such as cookies, puzzles, or toys, waiting to be discovered when the cracker breaks open.

Carolers and bell-ringers

Victorians revived the custom of Christmas caroling. They sang carols in church, at home, and while strolling from house to house with a group of friends. Carolers enjoyed treats and hot drinks at people's homes and collected gifts and money for the poor.

Other music makers also took to the streets. Beautiful melodies, played on hand bells, chimed through the air. Each bell had a different ring and, when played in a certain order, they made a song.

Wassailing

Wassailing is an ancient English custom that was renewed during Victorian times. Wassailing is wishing others good health by sharing with them a drink of hot punch called **wassail**. The punch contains sherry, cider, ale, lemons, spices, and roasted apples.

Families kept a bowl of wassail ready to be shared with visitors. Many carolers brought along their own wassail and, after a song, invited the family to enjoy a cup with them. The family then refilled the carolers' bowl with their own punch.

Christmas angels

Angels were an important part of Christmas celebrations. The Angel Gabriel told Mary that she would give birth to the Christ Child. When Jesus was born in Bethlehem, another angel, Raphael, appeared to shepherds in the fields and announced his birth. Raphael was joined by a choir of angels who sang praises to God. A popular Christmas carol recalls this happy time. Do you know these words? "Hark! The herald angels sing, glory to the newborn King..."

Angel hair
Some children believed that angels brought the tree and gifts at Christmastime. As the angels set up the tree, they left behind fine hair that resembled glistening cobwebs. This "angel hair," made from spun glass, decorated many Victorian Christmas trees. It was later replaced by tinsel.

Christmas angels and cherubs
People of the Victorian era had a great love of angels. They placed an angel either at or near the top of their Christmas tree. Angels known as **cherubs** were also popular during this time. Although cherubs were believed to be powerful angels, Victorian artists showed them as cute, chubby babies who resembled Cupid.

An end and a beginning

New Year's Eve parties allowed people to bid farewell to the old year and celebrate the coming of the new. People found many ways to bring in the new year.

First-footing

One popular new year's tradition was **first-footing**. The first man to step inside another person's home after midnight was the first-footer. He brought the family a piece of coal and wished everyone a "Happy New Year." First-footing was believed to bring the family good luck—but only if their first-footer had brown or black hair!

Mumming

Mumming is an old tradition that is still practiced in some places. People who took part in mumming were called **mummers** or **maskers**. Mummers went from house to house disguised in costumes, speaking in strange voices, and asking for food and drink. Mumming is still popular in Newfoundland. In Philadelphia, a mumming parade is held each year on New Year's Day.

Epiphany—the 12th Day of Christmas

The season's celebrations did not end on New Year's Day. People visited friends and enjoyed festive activities until **Epiphany** on January 6th. The Feast of the Epiphany celebrated the day the Three Wise Men arrived at the stable where Jesus was born. This holy day marked the end of the holiday season. People went to church, wrote thank-you notes, and took down their decorations. Families settled in for the rest of winter with warm memories of the Christmas that had just passed.

Make your own Christmas decorations

You can decorate your own Victorian tree! Look at the decorations inside the painted ornaments—they were all made by hand. Some were made using natural objects and resemble decorations hung on early trees. Some were made with fancier, store-bought items. They are similar to ornaments found on later Victorian trees.

Dried fruit decorations

You will need an apple and an orange, a knife, waxed paper, a baking sheet, narrow ribbon, and an adult to help you slice the fruit and use the oven.

Slice fruit across its core and spread slices on a baking sheet covered with waxed paper. Preheat oven to 65°C (150°F). Bake fruit between eight and twelve hours—until it feels leathery. When fruit is cool, get an adult to poke two small holes in each slice, using the tip of a knife. Pull one end of the ribbon through each hole and tie a bow at the front. Hang fruit ornament on tree.

Cornucopia

You will need a round paper doily, glue, and ribbon.

Fold doily in half, making a semicircle. Roll into cone shape and glue edge. Poke ribbon through one of the lacy holes and tie ends together. Fill cornucopia with small treats and hang on tree.

Lacy hearts

You will need lace, fabric or wallpaper, ribbon, stuffing, pins, and a stapler or needle and thread.

Pin two small pieces of fabric or wallpaper together and cut out a heart (you will have two pieces when you unpin the fabric or paper). Lay one heart with its "good" side facing down and put a line of glue around its edge. Place the lace in glue and leave it to dry. Next, staple or stitch hearts together, leaving a small opening for stuffing. Stuff heart and finish closing edges. Glue a loop of ribbon to the back and hang heart on tree.

Glossary

Advent The four weeks prior to Christmas

bale A tightly bound bundle

Bethlehem An ancient town, south of Jerusalem, in the Middle East

bishop A high-ranking priest in some Christian churches

blown glass Glass that is shaped by air blown through a tube

bough A large branch of a tree

cherub A type of angel that resembles a plump baby

Christmas box A Christmas present

Christmas piece A Christmas card made by children in school

Cupid A winged boy with a bow and arrows known in ancient times as the god of love

custom Something done so often that it has become an accepted practice

Epiphany The Twelfth Day of Christmas, when the Wise Men are said to have visited the baby Jesus

evergreen A tree or plant that keeps its green needles year round

garland A string of vines, flowers, and leaves that are tied together and hung as a decoration

hand-dipped Describes an item repeatedly submerged in a liquid such as melted wax

holly An evergreen plant with shiny jagged leaves and small red berries

Jesus Christ The name given to the Son of God in the Christian faith

manger A wooden trough used for feeding cattle or horses

Midnight Mass A Christmas Eve service that is celebrated by many Roman Catholics

miniature A tiny version of an object

mummer A person disguised in a mask or costume

Nativity The birth of Jesus Christ

nineteenth century The period of time between the years 1801 and 1900

ornate Describing something that is elaborately decorated

parlor The most formal room in a home, used for entertaining; also called salon or drawing room

sheaf A bundle of grain stalks

spun glass Glass that is blown into delicate threadlike fibers

traditional Describing customs or beliefs that are handed down from generation to generation

Victorian Describing the period of time between 1837 and 1901, when Queen Victoria ruled Britain; describing objects, styles, or people of this time

Index

Acknowledgments

Illustrations
All illustrations by Barbara Bedell except the following:
Louis Prang from the Hallmark Design Collections, Hallmark Cards Inc.: pages 16-17
Lisa Smith: page 22

Colorizations
Antoinette "Cookie" DeBiasi: page 8 (bottom)
Lynda Hale: page 8 (top)

Photographs and reproductions
Archive Photos/Fotos International TM: page 25
Bobbie Kalman: page 30

Special thanks to
Sharman Robertson and Hallmark Cards Inc., Jamie Maxwell and The Toronto Historical Board, Dundurn Castle, and The Gibson House Museum